Also by W. S. Merwin

THE PUPIL

THE PUPIL

POEMS BY *W. S. Merwin*

Alfred A. Knopf NEW YORK 2002

This Is a Borzoi Book Published by Alfred A. Knopf
Copyright © 2001 by W. S. Merwin

All rights reserved under International and Pan-American Copyright Conventions.
Published in the United States by Alfred A. Knopf, a division of Random House, Inc.,
New York, and simultaneously in Canada by Random House of Canada Limited, Toronto.
Distributed by Random House, Inc., New York.
www.randomhouse.com/knopf/poetry

Knopf, Borzoi Books, and the colophon are registered trademarks of Random House, Inc.

Some of these poems were originally published in the following periodicals:
The American Poetry Review: A Calling; Feast Day; The Marfa Lights;
Migrants by Night
The Atlantic: Any Time; Before the Flood; In the Open; The Sleeper; A Term; Unknown Bird
The Boston Review: Aliens; Unseen Touch
The Hudson Review: The Open Land; Sonnet
The Kenyon Review: Overtone
Literary Imagination: The Moment
Metre: Downstream (originally printed in a Getty Museum program)
The New York Review of Books: The Comet Museum (also appeared in Metre); Home Tundra;
Plan for the Death of Ted Hughes; The Summer; Through a Glass; Usage
The New Yorker: The Name of the Air
Painted Leaf Press: The Fence (also appeared in Metre)
The Paris Review: Before the May Fair; Daylight (also appeared in Metre);
The Hollow in the Stone; Once in Spring
The Partisan Review: The Youth of Animal
Poetry: Calling Late; Far Company; Good People; The Hours of Darkness; In Time; Just Now;
Mid-Air Mirror; The Night Plums; Prophecy; Remembering the Signs; The Time of Shadow;
Under the Day
Shenandoah: At Night Before Spring; Flights in the Dark
Slate: Lit in Passing; Memorandum: The Source;
To a Friend Who Keeps Telling Me That He Has Lost His Memory
Southen California Anthology: One Night in April
Tabla: Worn

Library of Congress Cataloging-in-Publication Data
Merwin, W. S. (William Stanley).
The pupil : poems / by W. S. Merwin.—1st ed.
p.   cm.
ISBN 0-375-70964-9
I. Title.
PS3563.E75 P86 2001
811'.54—dc21   2001033729
Manufactured in the United States of America
Published November 7, 2001
First Paperback Edition October 2002

For Paula

Contents

THE PUPIL

Prophecy

At the end of the year the stars go out
the air stops breathing and the Sibyl sings
first she sings of the darkness she can see
she sings on until she comes to the age
without time and the dark she cannot see

no one hears then as she goes on singing
of all the white days that were brought to us one
by one that turned to colors around us

a light coming from far out in the eye
where it begins before she can see it

burns through the words that no one has believed

The Comet Museum

So the feeling comes afterward
some of it may reach us only
long afterward when the moment
itself is beyond reckoning

beyond time beyond memory
as though it were not moving in
heaven neither burning farther
through any past nor ever to
arrive again in time to be
when it has gone the senses wake

all through the day they wait for it
here are pictures that someone took
of what escaped us at the time
only now can we remember

Sonnet

Where it begins will remain a question
for the time being at least which is to
say for this lifetime and there is no
other life that can be this one again
and where it goes after that only one
at a time is ever about to know
though we have it by heart as one and though
we remind each other on occasion

How often may the clarinet rehearse
alone the one solo before the one
time that is heard after all the others
telling the one thing that they all tell of
it is the sole performance of a life
come back I say to it over the waters

The Time of Shadow

This is the hour Marais told us about
some time in the days before we were born
while the sun went down over Africa
in the youth of the century and age
gathered upon him with the returning
black ceiling of morphine   Eugène Marais
watching our ancestors in the evening
our contemporaries in the strange world
their descendants had made as shadows reached
toward them he recognized in their shadow
a shadow of his own it was the time
for boasting before the end of the day
strutting and playing having decided
upon the sleeping place near the water
the time of the children playing swinging
by a rock pool and then the sun went down
and the voices fell silent and the games
were still and the old were overcome with
a great sadness and then the sounds of mourning
began for the whole loss without a name
he called it the hour of Hesperean
Melancholy but as he knew it could
visit at its own moment here it is
the choir loft in the church burned long ago
childhood in a blue robe and suddenly
no sound but the depth of loss unknown loss
irreparable and nameless and tears
with no word for them although there may be
playing again later in the darkness
even for a long time in the moonlight
and singing again out of the dark trees

The Hours of Darkness

When there are words
waiting in line once more
I find myself looking
into the eyes of an old
man I have seen before
who is holding a long white cane
as he stares past my head
talking of poems and youth

after him a shadow
where I thought to see a face
asks have you considered
how often you return
to the subject of not seeing
to the state of blindness
whether you name it or not
do you intend to speak of that
as often as you do
do you mean anything by it

I look up into the year
that the black queen could still see
the year of the alien lights
appearing to her and then going
away with the others
the year of the well of darkness
overflowing with no
moon and no stars

it was there all the time
behind the eye of day
Rumphius saw it before
he had words for anything
long before he wrote
of the hermit crab *These*
wanderers live in the houses
of strangers wondering
where they had come from
Vermeij in our time
never saw any creature
living or as a fossil
but can summon by touch
the story of a cowrie
four hundred million years old
scars ancestry and what
it knew in the dark sea

there Borges is talking
about Milton's sonnet
and Milton hears the words
of Samson to someone else
and Homer is telling
of a landscape without horizons
and the blind knight whom no one
ever could touch with a sword
says in my head there is
only darkness
so they never find me
but I know where they are

it is the light
that appears to change and be many
to be today
to flutter as leaves
to recognize the rings of the trees
to come again
one of the stars is from
the day of the cowrie
one is from a time in the garden
we see the youth of the light
in all its ages
we see it as bright
points of animals
made long ago out of night

how small the day is
the time of colors
the rush of brightness

Flights in the Dark

After nights of rain
the great moths of December
drift through green fronds
into the end of the year

I watch their eyes
on the door near midnight
memories of the sun
near the solstice

and their wings made of darkness
the memory of darkness
flying in time
remembering this night

The Marfa Lights

Are they there in the daytime
east of town on the way to Paisano Pass
rising unseen by anyone
climbing in long arcs over Mitchell Flat
candles at noon being carried
by hands never named never caught on film
never believed as they go up the long stairs
of the light to glide in secret or dance
along the dazzling halls out of sight
above where the air shimmers like a sea

only when the curtain of light
is fading thin above the black Glass Mountains
and the first stars are glittering
do the claims of sightings begin
they may occur from anywhere facing
the removes of those broken horizons
though most of them nowadays
are likely to come from somewhere on Route 90
looking south toward the Chinatis
a marker has been set up by the road there

and cars begin to stop before
sundown pulling over into the lay-by
designated with rimrocks folding chairs
are unlimbered while there is still light
and positioned among the piled stones at spots
expecting them as niches along
sea cliffs expect their old fishermen
tripods are set up and telescopes
they all seem to know what they are waiting for

then buses with lines of faces
peering over each other at the windows
at one time out there was the place to take
a date it used to mean something different
if you said you had been out to see
the lights but almost everybody
had seen them whether or not they had
seen just the same things and all were shadowed by
the same explanations there were reports
of those lights before there were cars or ranches

they were seen over wagon trains
on their way up from the valley and seen shining
above the bare moving forests
of cattle horns in the pass sometimes a light
would drift and swell and suddenly
shudder and fly up bursting apart from one
color to another some say
they will turn out to be something simple
a trick of the atmosphere
and some do not think they are anything

insisting that people will believe
whatever they want to in the same way
that herdsmen and cowhands in the Chinatis
for a hundred years would whisper
that the lights were the ghost of the war chief
Alsate who had been captured
and dragged off to his death and his followers
sold into slavery of course
by now there have been investigations

inconclusive until the present
telling us in our turn what we do not know
what the evidence amounts to
perhaps and how far the theories have gone
to suggest what these bright appearances
portend in the eye of the mind where we know
from the beginning that the darkness
is beyond us there is no explaining
the dark it is only the light
that we keep feeling a need to account for

Migrants by Night

Weeks after the solstice
now in the winter night
the roar of surf thunders
from the foot of the sea cliffs
the heavy swells crashing
after their voyages
out of the deep north
the roar lifts from them
to roll on without them
as they break in the foam
of the ones before them
with that sound under them
carrying the mountain
into the midst of the sea

which they have always been
since the first motion
that was in no place then
out of no place began
gathering itself in turn
to become a direction
under the clear wind
from the place of origin
that now lifts the thin
swift cries of the plovers
over the dark ocean
each one calling alone
unseen to hear again
another in the wind

in a season between
journeys with no horizon
they fly in the night
as though it could be known
from season to season
as though it were their own
to hear each other in
while it turns around them
and the waves of light flow in
from the first motion
bringing it with them
all the way to the moment
when the cry comes again
again before it flies on

In the Open

Those summer nights when the planes came over
it seemed it was every night that summer
after the still days of perfect weather
I kept telling myself what it was not
that I was feeling as the afternoon
light deepened into the lingering
radiance that colored its leaving us
that was the light through which I would come home
again and again with the day over
picking my way from Whitehall through the new
rubble in the known streets the broken glass
signaling from among the crevices
fallen facades hoses among the mounds
figures in rubber coming and going
at the ruins or gathered with lowered
voices they all spoke in lowered voices
as I recall now so that all I heard
was the murmured current I can still hear
how many in that building I might hear
something like that how many in that one
then a quiet street the shop doors open
figures waiting in lines without a word
with the night ahead no it was not fear
I said to myself that was not the word
for whatever I heard as the door closed
as we talked of the day as we listened
as the fork touched the plate like a greeting
as the curtains were drawn as the cat stretched
as the news came on with word of losses
warning of the night as we picked up the ground sheet
and the folded blankets as I bent down
to remember the fur of Tim the cat
as the door closed and the stairs in the dark
led us back down to the street and the night
swung wide before us once more in the park

Often after the all-clear it would be
very cold suddenly a reminder
hardly more than that as I understood
of the great cold of the dark everywhere
around us deeper than I could believe
usually she was asleep by then
warm and breathing softly I could picture
how she must look the long curve of her lips
the high white forehead I wondered about
her eyelids and what calm they had come to
while the ice reached me much of the night was
in pieces by then behind me piled up
like rubble all fallen into the same
disorder the guns shouting from the hill
the drones and the broad roar of planes the screams
of sirens the pumping of bombs coming
closer the beams groping over the smoke
they all seemed to have ended somewhere without
saying this is the last one you seldom
hear the dog stop barking there were people
on all sides of us in the park asleep
awake the sky was clear I lay looking
up into it through the cold to the lights
the white moments that had traveled so long
each one of them to become visible
to us then only for that time and then
where did they go in the dark afterward
the invisible dark the cold never
felt or ever to be felt where was it
then as I lay looking up into all
that had been coming to pass and was still
coming to pass some of the stars by then
were nothing but the light that had left them
before there was life on earth and nothing
would be seen after them and the light from
one of them would have set out exactly
when the first stir of life recognized death
and began its delays that light had been

on its way from there all through what happened
afterward through the beginning of pain
the return of pain into the senses
into feelings without words and then words
traveling toward us even in our sleep
words for the feelings of those who are not
there now and words we say are for ourselves
then sounds of feet went by in the damp grass
dark figures slipping away toward morning

Overtone

Some listening were certain they could hear
through the notes summoned from the strings one more
following at a distance low but clear
a resonance never part of the score
not noticed during the rehearsals nor
prayed into the performance and yet here
with the first note it had been waiting for
holding silent the iced minors of fear
the key of grief the mourning from before
the names were read of those no longer there
that sound of what made no sound any more
made up the chords that in a later year
some still believed that they could overhear
echoing music played during a war

Fires in Childhood

That Sunday we drove home through the mountains
it was gray spring Easter the trees still bare
by the river my father was somewhere
in England the radio on for once
each fading station crackling the same news
through paper far off the bombs coming down
behind the voices all night on London
the city burning and the searchlight rays
groping up through the smoke St. Paul's was still
untouched though waves of bombs went on falling
I kept seeing Alice roller skating
and close to me on the piano stool
whom my fat cousin claimed he found sitting
on the floor once so he saw everything

Glassy Sea

As you see each of the stars has a voice
and at least one long syllable before
words as we know them and can recall them
later one by one with their company
around them after the sound of them has
gone from its moment even though we may
say it again and again it is gone
again far into our knowledge there are
words as we know for whatever does not
die with us but the sound of those words lasts
no longer than the others it is heard
only for part of the length of a breath
among those clear syllables never heard
from which the words were made in another
time and the syllables themselves are not
there forever some may go all the way
to the beginning but not beyond it

The Moment

In the country in which I was a child
in an age some time before mine they found
a black river sleeping deep in the ground
stream of black glass veined current of night stone
old to the touch and they believed it was
for them to burn though the ones who woke it
died of it in the sunlight by their doors
breath sifting the blackened days still it was
broken like glass and gleamed like the surface
of a river older than the river
and was polished as an eye but an eye
from the sleep this side of the diamond
taking from the light of the present
nothing that we can tell or that we see
not noticing everything that has gone
but staring at what has yet to happen

Any Time

How long ago the day is
when at last I look at it
with the time it has taken
to be there still in it
now in the transparent light
with the flight in the voices
the beginning in the leaves
everything I remember
and before it before me
present at the speed of light
in the distance that I am
who keep reaching out to it
seeing all the time faster
where it has never stirred from
before there is anything
the darkness thinking the light

Far Company

At times now from some margin of the day
I can hear birds of another country
not the whole song but a brief phrase of it
out of a music that I may have heard
once in a moment I appear to have
forgotten for the most part that full day
no sight of which I can remember now
though it must have been where my eyes were then
that knew it as the present while I thought
of somewhere else without noticing that
singing when it was there and still went on
whether or not I noticed now it falls
silent when I listen and leaves the day
and flies before it to be heard again
somewhere ahead when I have forgotten

Aliens

When they appeared on the terrace soon after daybreak
high above the sea with the tide far out I thought at first
they were sparrows which by now seem to have found their
    way everywhere
following us at their own small distances arguing over
pieces of our shadows to take up into their brief flights
eluding our attention by seeming unremarkable
quick instantaneous beyond our grasp as they are in
    themselves
complete lives flashing from the beginning each eye bearing
the beginning in its dusty head and even their voices
seemed at first to be the chatter of sparrows half small talk half
    bickering
but no when I looked more closely they were linnets the
    brilliant
relatives the wanderers out of another part of the story
with their heads the colors of the ends of days and that
    unsoundable
gift for high delicate headlong singing that has rung
even out of vendors' cages when the morning light has
    touched them

Mid-Air Mirror

When I looked across the river
to where we are sitting talking
quietly in the high white room
through the late winter afternoon
old friends found after a long time

what I saw from that end of time
was only the light reflected
on all the buildings facing west
the Metropolitan Tower
white and the brick cliffs glittering
high beyond the green ferry barns
and untouched day where we are now

the ferry barns have disappeared
and ferries passing back and forth
on the loom of fine river light
while we have pursued a notion
that we were learning as we turned

among the galaxies learning
we called it as we recognized
some place we were and the known light
sometimes voices of friends again
but not ourselves the dark of space
not ourselves yet the farthest light

A Term

At the last minute a word is waiting
not heard that way before and not to be
repeated or ever be remembered
one that always had been a household word
used in speaking of the ordinary
everyday recurrences of living
not newly chosen or long considered
or a matter for comment afterward
who would ever have thought it was the one
saying itself from the beginning through
all its uses and circumstances to
utter at last that meaning of its own
for which it had long been the only word
though it seems now that any word would do

Unspoken Greeting

Morning without number not yet knowing of such things
coming out before anything to the eyes of birds
hushed light before the sun brings back the reflections of
    syllables
cool instant when the colors lie deep in a breath before meaning
presence never identified given back now altogether
out of the unbroken dark and the beams of stars that were not
    there
behind the whole of night out of their light you appear once
rising through yourself in stillness at the speed of starlight
while the dragonfly hovers above the glassy pond
on its wings of veined sky before occurrence or mention
boundless morning not ever to be approached or believed or
    seen again

The Open Land

Mist iridescent over the rice fields
mountains far away those gray fish running
so that they scarcely seem to be moving
rolled hay camped nearby in shaven meadows
sleeping into winter as the roads sleep
into themselves into their unseen age
leading the whole of their lives while the light
appears always to come from just before
so that all of it seems to be familiar
known in passing like clouds but the only
words for it are ways to tell of distance

Before the Flood

Why did he promise me
that we would build ourselves
an ark all by ourselves
out in back of the house
on New York Avenue
in Union City New Jersey
to the singing of the streetcars
after the story
of Noah whom nobody
believed about the waters
that would rise over everything
when I told my father
I wanted us to build
an ark of our own there
in the backyard under
the kitchen could we do that
he told me that we could
I want to I said and will we
he promised me that we would
why did he promise that
I wanted us to start then
nobody will believe us
I said that we are building
an ark because the rains
are coming and that was true
nobody ever believed
we would build an ark there
nobody would believe
that the waters were coming

A Calling

My father is telling me the story of Samuel
not for the first time and yet he is not quite repeating
nor rehearsing nor insisting he goes on telling me
in the empty green church smelling of carpet and late dust
where he calls to mind words of the prophets to mumble in a
    remote language
and the prophets are quoting the Lord who is someone they
    know
who has been talking to them my father tells what the Lord
said to them and Samuel listened and heard someone calling
    someone
and Samuel answered Here I am and my father is saying
that is the answer that should be given he is telling me
that someone is calling and that is the right answer
he is telling me a story he wants me to believe
telling me the right answer and the way it was spoken
in that story he wants to believe in which someone is calling

Remembering the Signs

My father took me to Coney Island
that one time because it was closed or on
the point of closing a day past the end
of summer and the hot busy season
so we could see the place it had happened
up until then where the rides had begun
into that silence gates had shut behind
he told me how dangerous they had been
even if we had come when they opened
there was not one on which we would have gone
nor paid for tickets into the darkened
side shows to look at what should not be seen
it was enough he said to walk around
getting to see it just as it was then

Lit in Passing

In the first sound of their own feet
on the steps outside the empty
house they might have heard it under
the talk that day as it told them
in a language they pretended
not to understand a word of

here begins the hollow to come

presenting itself as a small
triumph before he turned forty
the big house twelve echoing rooms
thirty-six windows that would need
curtains my mother said at once
and the huge church across the street

everything to be done over
fresh and new at the beginning
in those first milk and honey days
even new stained glass windows made
downstairs on the long tables of
the church kitchen the webs of lead
and gray glass waiting for the light

they even made one at that time
for the house the manse a window
over the landing on the stairs
halfway up my mother never
liked it she did not explain why
there was a shield with a ruby
at the center a red point climbed
up the stairs through the afternoon
marked us as we went up and down

those last years we were together

At Night Before Spring

Two nights before the equinox that will
turn into spring in the dark the next time
before the last spring in a thousand years
as we count them I find myself looking
at the transparent indigo humor
that we called the night back in the daytime
and I see beyond acceleration
each of the lights complete in its own time
in the stillness of motion the stillness
with no beginning all in one moment
a friend beside me whom I do not see
without words making it come clear to me
the youth of heaven the ages of light
each of them whole in the unmoving blue
each with its number known in the unknown
each with its only self in the one eye
even as I watch it we are passing
the numbers are rising as I am told
they will rise and it will be spring again
it seems that I have forgotten nothing
I believe I have not lost anyone

One Night in April

Tonight no sound
of any bird
second night after
the full moon
only the wind now
I think the plovers
must have flown
I see the silver
clouds crossing the moon
out of the east
northeast
moving fast
a day ago
I heard them
fly over calling
and a night ago
they were still here
I heard them overhead
but by now they are
maybe a thousand
miles on their way
northward over
the dark of the ocean
as they fly they are
calling those two
notes now too far
tonight to hear

Unknown Bird

Out of the dry days
through the dusty leaves
far across the valley
those few notes never
heard here before

one fluted phrase
floating over its
wandering secret
all at once wells up
somewhere else

and is gone before it
goes on fallen into
its own echo leaving
a hollow through the air
that is dry as before

where is it from
hardly anyone
seems to have noticed it
so far but who now
would have been listening

it is not native here
that may be the one
thing we are sure of
it came from somewhere
else perhaps alone

so keeps on calling for
no one who is here
hoping to be heard
by another of its own
unlikely origin

trying once more the same few
notes that began the song
of an oriole last heard
years ago in another
existence there

it goes again tell
no one it is here
foreign as we are
who are filling the days
with a sound of our own

Daylight

It is said that after he was seventy
Ingres returned to the self-portrait
he had painted at twenty-four and he
went on with it from that far off though
there was no model and in the mirror
only the empty window and gray sky
and the light in which his hand was lifted
a hand which the eyes in the painting would not
have recognized at first raised in a way
they would never see whatever he might
bring to them nor would they ever see him
as he had come to be then watching them
there where he had left them and while he looked
into them from no distance as he thought
holding the brush in the day between them

Worn

Then what I come back to now is
an age that I could not have seen
until this time and as others
I knew did not live to see it
but where is it at this moment
in spring when the morning shows me
again what I thought I had known
for so long the river taking
its time the stones lifted out
of the ground and set into walls
for a while waiting to return
the tools passed from hand to hand
keeping the shine of the handles
the hollows of the stone doorsills
polished as though they were daylight
so that I step over them to
turn into the time I go through

Downstream

Those two for whom two rivers had been named
how could it be that nobody knew them
nobody had seen them nobody seemed
to have anything to say about them
or maybe even to believe in them
if I asked who was Juniata who
was Marietta finding their names on
the map again feeling my throat tighten
and a day growing warmer in my chest
if I heard their names so I knew they were
secret and I was silent when we traveled
when we came close to them and caught sight
of the skin of water under the bending
trees the curves where they came out of hiding
and every time always they were different
always in secret they were beautiful
they had been waiting for me before I
heard they were there and they knew everything
Juniata was older sometimes and
sometimes a girl a late day in summer
a longed-for homecoming Marietta
was a little ahead of me waiting
and shy about nothing taking my hand
showing me and what has become of them
who would believe now what they were like once
nobody can remember the rivers

Before the May Fair

Last night with our minds still in cold April
in the late evening we watched the river
heavy with the hard rains of the recent spring
as it wheeled past wrapped in its lowered note
by the gray walls at the foot of the streets
through the gray twilight of this season
the cars vanished one by one unnoticed
folded away like animals and last
figures walking dogs went in and shutters
closed gray along gray houses leaving
the streets empty under the cries of swifts
turning above the chimneys the trailers
parked under the trees by the riverbank
stood as though they were animals asleep
while the animals standing in the trucks
were awake stirring and the animals
waiting in the slaughterhouse were awake
the geese being fattened with their feet nailed
to the boards were awake as the small lights
went out over doorways and the river
slipped through the dark time under the arches
of the stone bridge restored once more after
the last war the bells counted the passing
hours one sparrow all night by a window
kept saying This This This until the streets
were the color of dark clouds and under
the trees in the cold down by the river
the first planks were laid out across the trestles
and cold hands piled them for the coming day

Once in Spring

A sentence continues after thirty years
it wakes in the silence of the same room
the words that come to it after the long comma
existed all that time wandering in space
as points of light travel unseen through ages
of which they alone are the measure and arrive
at last to tell of something that came to pass
before they ever began or meant anything

longer ago than that Pierre let himself in
through the gate under the cherry tree and said
Jacques is dead and his feet rustled the bronze leaves
of the cherry tree the October leaves fallen
before he set out to walk on their curled summer
then as suddenly Pierre was gone without warning
and the others all the others who were announced
after they had gone with what they had of their summer
and the cherry tree was done and went the way of its
    leaves

as they wake in the sentence the words remember
but each time only a remnant and it may be
that they say little and there is the unspoken
morning late in spring the early light passing
and the cuckoo hiding beyond its voice and once more
the oriole that was silent from age to age
voices heard once only and then long listened for

The Veil of May

No more than a week and the leaves
have all come out on the ash trees
now they are more than half open
on the ancient walnuts standing
alone in the field reaching up
through the mute amazement of age
they have uncurled on the oaks from
hands small as the eyelids of birds
and the morning light shines through them
and waits while the hawthorn gleams white
against the green in the shadow
in a moment the river has
disappeared down in the valley
the curve of sky gliding slowly
from before not seeming to move
it will not be seen again now
a while from this place on the ridge
but over it the summer will
flow and not seem to be moving

The Youth of Animals

They start by learning to listen
for the approach of the first time
ages before their eyes open
upon the night that holds them
younger than the night they had known
which was always whole and unseen
and then they see the first light come
to find them and when it knows them
they call out for it is the one
that they knew before they began

then what happens is the first time
and they see it all around them
as they know the song of hunger
repeating the notes of its climb
out of them and hear the answer
coming back to its only name
the way one after the other
the days come back to the same
faces where they have lived before
and find them again the first time

there was never a time before
but each day the eyes are wider
and the horizon tempts them more
whenever they see it again
one morning they wander farther
out toward it than ever before
not sure what they have come for
and then they come to the first time
and before they know it are gone
that one time and the time after

The Hollow in the Stone

Not every kind of water will do
to make the pool under the rock face
that afterward will be clear forever

not the loud current of great event
already far downstream in its moment
heavy with the dark waste of cities
not the water of falling
with its voice far away from it
not the water that ran with the days
and runs with them now

only the still water
that we can see through all the way
whatever we remember
the clear water from before
that was there under the reflections
of the leaves in spring and beyond
and under the clouds passing below them

Late Song

Long evening at the end of spring
with soft rain falling and flowing
from the eaves into the broken
stone basin outside the window
a blackbird warning of nightfall
coming and I hear it again
announcing that it will happen
darkness and the day will be gone
as I heard it all years ago
knowing no more than I know now
but once more I sit and listen
in the same still room to the rain
at the end of spring and again
hear the blackbird in the evening

The Source

There in the fringe of trees between
the upper field and the edge of the one
below it that runs above the valley
one time I heard in the early
days of summer the clear ringing
six notes that I knew were the opening
of the Fingal's Cave Overture
I heard them again and again that year
and the next summer and the year
afterward those six descending
notes the same for all the changing
in my own life since the last time
I had heard them fall past me from
the bright air in the morning of a bird
and I believed that what I had heard
would always be there if I came again
to be overtaken by that season
in that place after the winter
and I would wonder again whether
Mendelssohn really had heard them somewhere
far to the north that many years ago
looking up from his youth to listen to
those six notes of an ancestor
spilling over from a presence neither
water nor human that led to the cave
in his mind the fluted cliffs and the wave
going out and the falling water
he thought those notes could be the music for
Mendelssohn is gone and Fingal is gone
all but his name for a cave and for one
piece of music and the black-capped warbler
as we called that bird that I remember
singing there those notes descending
from the age of the ice dripping
I have not heard again this year can it

be gone then will I not hear it
from now on will the overture begin
for a time and all those who listen
feel that falling in them but as always
without knowing what they recognize

First Sight

There once more the new moon in spring
above the roofs of the village
in the clear sky the cold twilight
under the evening star the thin
shell sinking so lightly it seems
not to be moving and no sound
from the village at this moment
nor from the valley below it
with its still river nor even
from any of the birds and I
have been standing here in this light
seeing this moon and its one star
while the cows went home with their bells
and the sheep were folded and gone
and the elders fell silent one
after another and loved souls
were no longer seen and my hair
turned white and I was looking up
out of a time of late blessings

First of June

Night when the south wind wakes the owl
and the owl says it is summer
now it is time to be summer
it is time for that departure
though the blanket dates from childhood
it is time whoever you are
to be going they are older
every one of them there is spring
no longer this is the south wind
you have heard about that brings rain
taking away roofs with a breath
and a season of grapes in one
blind unpredictable moment
of hail this is the white wind that
you cannot believe here it is
and the owl sails out to see whose
turn it is tonight to be changed

Unseen Touch

Surprised again in the dark by the sound of rain
falling slowly steadily a reassurance
after all with no need to say anything
in spite of the memories of dust and the parched waiting
the green lost and the slow bleaching out of the hills
here is the known hand again knowing remembering
at night after the doubting and the news of age

The Summer

After we come to see it and
know we scarcely live without it
we begin trying to describe
what art is and it seems to be
something we believe is human
whatever that is something that
says what we are but then the same
beam of recognition stops at
one penguin choosing a pebble
to offer to the penguin he
hopes to love and later the dance
of awkwardness holding an egg
on one foot away from the snow
of summer the balancing on
one foot in the flash of summer

The Black Virgin

You are not part of knowing are you
at the top of the stairs in the white cliff
in the deep valley smelling of summer
you are not part of vanity although
it may have climbed up on its knees to you
and paid to be a name cut on the way
you do not need the candles before you
you would not see them I suppose if you
were to open your eyelids you are not
seen in what is visible it appears
and the crown is not part of you whatever
it is made of nor the robe of days
with its colors glittering you are not
part of pride or owning or understanding
and the questions that have been carried to you
life after life lie there unseen at your feet
oh presence in silence while the dark swifts
flash past with one cry out in the sunlight

To the Spiders of This Room

You who waited here before me
in silence mothers of silence
I always knew you were present
whether or not I could see you
in your gray clouds your high corners
spinners of the depths of shadows

who recur without memory
rising from beneath the moment
as it breathes trembles and is gone
bearers of a message not known
heirs of an unseen lineage

this is the moment to thank you
for ever appearing to me
through these years keepers of no word
attentive in this mute room while
the bird sang and the rain murmured
and the voice echoed from the road

patient guardians who revealed
in each sound the hour of the fly

Above the Long Field

Those lives of which I know nothing
though I stand at the same window
watching a day in the old tree
the constellations in daylight
and hear one bird with the short song

those are things they too must have known
so they have been gone a long time
and by the time I come to them
already they are far away
notes of sheep bells on the last day
those sheep wore them threading the lane
without knowing that there would be
no more of those days and I heard
them go but did not know that then

it was a quiet day like this
clear and still as I recall it
with a few voices carrying
from a long way a day in spring
I think it was although I know
that it happened too in autumn

an hour like this before the white
sky of summer or the white hill
of winter a day in color
but in unremembered colors

Under the Day

To come back like autumn
to the moss on the stones
after many seasons
to recur as a face
backlit on the surface
of a dark pool one day
after the year has turned
from the summer it saw
while the first yellow leaves
stare from their forgetting
and the branches grow spare

is to waken backward
down through the still water
knowing without touching
all that was ever there
and has been forgotten
and recognize without
name or understanding
without believing or
holding or direction
in the way that we see
at each moment the air

Simon's Vision

After his youth Simon went south
in search of it thinking of bees
in September and hills of thyme
gray and shining and the winter
light under glass on long tables
in the damp of a nursery
wild geraniums cyclamens
the still bells of campanulas
and a beautiful witch and he
found all of them and now I wish
I had gone to see them in their
house up in the cliff according
to his directions at the time
for in a while the world Simon
had come to began to show through
so that he saw the other side
and this one where the colors are
and the flowers rise and we know
the same words he said all his life
looks to him like the stars at noon
though all is what it was before
blood of trees sugar in the dark
the idea of leaves in sleep
birds flying over an airport
finally turning into clouds
before we can really see them

Wings

Among my friends here is an old man named
for the first glimpse of light before daybreak
he teaches flying that is to say he
is able to fly himself and has taught
others to fly and for them it is their
only treasure but he has not taught me
though I dream of flying I fly in dreams
but when I see him he tells me of plants
he has saved for me and where they came from
a new one each time they have leaves like wings
like many wings some with wings like whole flocks
but they never fly he says or almost
never though there are some that can and do
but when they fly it is their only treasure
he says that if he taught me now to fly
it would be one treasure among others
just one among others is what he says
and he will wait he tells me and he speaks
of his old friends instead and their meetings
at intervals at a place where they fought
a battle long ago when they were young
and won and the ancient forest there was
destroyed as they fought but when they return
it rises again to greet them as though
no harm had ever come to it and while
they are there it spreads its wings over them

A Morning in Autumn

Here late into September
I can sit with the windows
of the stone room swung open
to the plum branches still green
above the two fields bare now
fresh-plowed under the walnuts
and watch the screen of ash trees
and the river below them

and listen to the hawk's cry
over the misted valley
beyond the shoulder of woods
and to lambs in a pasture
on the slope and a chaffinch
somewhere down in the sloe hedge
and silence from the village
behind me and from the years

and can hear the light rain come
the note of each drop playing
into the stone by the sill
I come slowly to hearing
then all at once too quickly
for surprise I hear something
and think I remember it
and will know it afterward

in a few days I will be
a year older one more year
a year farther and nearer
and with no sound from there on
mute as the native country
that was never there again
now I hear walnuts falling
in the country I came to

The Night Plums

Years afterward in the dark
in the middle of winter I saw them again
the sloes on the terraces
flowering in the small hours
after a season of hard cold and the turning
of the night and of the year and of years
when almost all whom I had known there
in other days had gone
and the stones of the barnyard were buried
in sleep and the animals were no more
I watched the white blossoms open
in their own hour naked and luminous
greeting the darkness in silence
with their ancient fragrance

In the Old Vineyard

That was a winter of last times
waking upstairs in the cold
empty house of the master
of San Beltran with its new floors
of imitation marble
its bare rooms living with echoes
though the window had been open
all night to another cold
that came down from the mountains
bringing the sound of sheep bells
from somewhere among the clouds
and before the sun was up
I would open the front door
as the fishermen my neighbors
were bringing the night catch
up the stairs to spread out
on the gray stones of the hour
then as the first rays kindled
the upper terraces
across the valley I heard
every morning the same
voice of a girl singing
her flight of notes that rose
along the tiers of stone
to touch the whole morning
with their hovering song
older than I could know

Just Now

In the morning as the storm begins to blow away
the clear sky appears for a moment and it seems to me
that there has been something simpler than I could ever
    believe
simpler than I could have begun to find words for
not patient not even waiting no more hidden
than the air itself that became part of me for a while
with every breath and remained with me unnoticed
something that was here unnamed unknown in the days
and the nights not separate from them
not separate from them as they came and were gone
it must have been here neither early nor late then
by what name can I address it now holding out my thanks

To a Friend Who Keeps Telling Me
That He Has Lost His Memory

And yet you know that you remember me
whoever I am and it is to me
you speak as you used to and we are sure of it

and you remember the child being saved
by some kind of mother from whatever
she insists he will never be able
to do when he has done it easily
the light has not changed at all on that one
falling in front of you as you look through it

and decades of explaining are a fan
that opens against the light here and there
proving something that then darkens again
they are at hand but even closer than they are
is the grandmother who entrusted you
with her old Baedecker to take along
on the Normandy landing where it turned out
to have powers and a time of its own

but the names fade out leaving the faces
weddings and processions anonymous
where is it that the sudden tears well up from
as you see faces turning in silence
though if they were here now it would still be
hard for you to hear what they said to you

and you lean forward and confide in me
as when you arrived once at some finely
wrought conclusion in the old days
that what interests you most of all now is birdsong
you have a plan to take some birds with you

Planh for the Death of Ted Hughes

There were so many streets then in London
they were always going to be there
there were more than enough to go all the way
there were so many days to walk through them
we would be back with the time of year
just as we were in the open day

there were so many words as we went on walking
sometimes three of us sometimes two
half the sentences flying unfinished
as we turned up the collars that had been through the wars
autumn in the park spring on the hill
winter on the bridges under what we started to say

there was so much dew even in Boston
even in the bright fall so many planets poised
on the sills of transparent houses it was coming to pass
around us the whole time before it happened
before the hearts stopped one after the other
and the silent wailing began that would not end

we were going to catch up with some of the sentences
in France or Idaho we were going
to shake them out again and listen
to what had not been caught by history or geography
or touched at all by the venomous weather
it was only a question of where and when

A Collection

After you were gone we found the garden
asking our way they all knew about it
we climbed out of town along the ravine
crossed the small bridge in the winter sunlight
came to the high wall and the parched gray door
knocked and heard nothing nothing knocked again
louder and heard the dripping of water
and nothing but knocked one more time and then
rubber boots on cement and the old man
your gardener coming from watering
the orchids motionless in their shelters
on their walls as he does every morning
though most of them are dormant at this time
but your green *Laelia digbyana*
was blooming reigning over a kingdom
in exile and by the house door I saw
two dogs shepherds staying where you left them

A Death in the Desert

for Bruce McGrew

You left just as the stars were beginning to go
the colors came back without you
you left us the colors
sand and rocks and the shades of late summer

Calling Late

Oh white lemurs who invented the dance
this is the time afterward
can you hear me
who invented the story

part of the story

oh blind lemurs who invented the morning
who touched the day
who held it aloft when it was early
who taught it to fly
can you hear the story

can you see now

oh shining lemurs who invented the beginning
who brought it along with you all the way
throwing it high up catching it never letting it fall
throwing it ahead throwing it far overhead
leaping up to it climbing into it

going to sleep in it shutting your eyes
with it safe inside them
are you listening

to the story
it has no beginning

One of the Laws

So it cannot be done to live
without being the cause of death
we know it in our blood running
unacknowledged even by us
we know it in each of our dreams
and in the new day's rising we
recognize it one more time
address it by another name

it is the need to tell ourselves
how it is not our fault that makes
it more terrible the hunger
to pardon ourselves because of
who we are the earnest belief
that we have a right to it from
somewhere because we deserve one

that brings up the pain of birth to
become cruelty and raises
story upon story cities
to indifference denying
existence to most suffering
while living off it kept alive
by it called by it from moment
to moment and by the right name

Star

All the way north on the train the sun
followed me followed me without moving
still the sun of that other morning
when we had gone over Come on over
men at the screen door said to my father
You have to see this it's an ape bring
the little boy bring the boy along

so he brought me along to the field
of dry grass hissing behind the houses
in the heat that morning and there was
nothing else back there but the empty day
above the grass waving as far away
as I could see and the sight burned my eyes
white birds were flying off beyond us

and a raised floor of boards like a house
with no house on it part way out there
was shining by itself a color
of shadow and the voices of the men
were smaller in the field as we walked on
something was standing out there on the floor
the men kept saying Come on over

it's on a chain and my father said
to me Don't get too close I saw it was
staring down at each of our faces
one after the other as though it might
catch sight of something in one of them
that it remembered I stood watching its eyes
as they turned away from each of us

in the burning day See it has its
bucket of water one of the men said
and that's higher than the dogs can get
but you wouldn't want to go up near it
I have to be careful bringing its food
keep out of reach sometimes it will swing that
chain and take to shrieking so it would

scare you unless you knew what it was
no way of telling how old it would be
but they don't live too long anyway
the heat was shimmering over the grass
as we left and it stood up straight watching us
until we were too far for it to see
and were gone already on our journey

Feast Day

Almost at the end of the century
this is the time of the pain of the bears
their agony goes on at this moment
for the amusement of the wedding guests
though the bears are harder to find by now
in the mountain forests of Pakistan
they cost more than they used to which makes it
all the more lavish and once they are caught
their teeth are pulled out and their claws pulled out
and among the entertainments after
the wedding one of them is hauled in now
and chained to a post and the dogs let loose
to hang on its nose so that the guests laugh
at the way it waves and dances and those
old enough to have watched this many times
compare it with other performances
saying they can tell from the way the bear
screams something about the children to be
born of the couple sitting there smiling
you may not believe it but the bear does

Good People

From the kindness of my parents
I suppose it was that I held
that belief about suffering

imagining that if only
it could come to the attention
of any person with normal
feelings certainly anyone
literate who might have gone

to college they would comprehend
pain when it went on before them
and would do something about it
whenever they saw it happen
in the time of pain the present
they would try to stop the bleeding
for example with their hands

but it escapes their attention
or there may be reasons for it
the victims under the blankets
the meat counters the maimed children
the animals the animals
staring from the end of the world

The Fence

for Matthew Shepard

This was what the west was won for
and this was the way it was won
but things were not like the old days
no Indians left to shoot at
a long time since the last bounties
on their kind no more wolves to hang
and stand next to for the picture
nothing left by the time they had
their first guns but the little things
running in front of them maybe
a hawk for the barn door if they
were lucky or a coyote
to string up on the barbed wire fence
which was what the fences were for
but they were growing up thinking
there had to be something better
it was time to find somebody
like themselves but different
in a way they could give a name to
point at make fun of and frighten
somebody who would understand
why it was happening to him
when he was tied to the barbed wire
which was what the fence was there for
and when he was beaten until
they thought it was time to leave him
and they drove away growing up

The Sleeper

On one of the last days of the installation in darkness
of the unlit procession that would continue its motionless march
to the end of the world and beyond it staring at nothing
after a ceremony during which mouths were opened
repeatedly but no words were shouted sung or spoken
the dog was carried into the tomb between two lines of bearers
followed by an orchestra holding silent instruments
and was lowered slowly into its far corner of that day's light
a sleeping dog not a guardian not a living dog
not a dog that had lived until then or had ever been born
a dog known from some life that would not be known again
the sculptor was the first in one file of bearers
and the sculptor's hand was the last to touch the figure
asleep in clay before they left it to its own sleep
and were blindfolded and turned around like planets and they
    groped
along the procession of horses chariots armor
to the light they remembered and the smells of smoke and
    cooking
then voices dogs barking dogs running among houses the
    sculptor
watched dogs searching and knowing what they were looking for
dogs asleep seeing somewhere else while his eye was on them

In Time

The night the world was going to end
when we heard those explosions not far away
and the loudspeakers telling us
about the vast fires on the backwater
consuming undisclosed remnants
and warning us over and over
to stay indoors and make no signals
you stood at the open window
the light of one candle back in the room
we put on high boots to be ready
for wherever we might have to go
and we got out the oysters and sat
at the small table feeding them
to each other first with the fork
then from our mouths to each other
until there were none and we stood up
and started to dance without music
slowly we danced around and around
in circles and after a while we hummed
when the world was about to end
all those years all those nights ago

Through a Glass

My face in the train window no color
years later taking me by surprise
when remembered looking older of course
behind it the fields I had known that long
flashing through it once again before I could
catch them the afternoon light the small lane
swinging by where an old man was walking
with a dog and their shadows while the face
raced past without moving and was neither
the daylight going nor the sight of it
once a snake left its whole skin by my door
still rustling without breath without a sound
all of a piece a shade out in the air
the silent rings in which a life had journeyed

Before Morning

A name in the dark a tissue of echoes

a breath repeated on the arch of my foot
the mute messenger
last one to have heard the music

I remember them saying
that I used to wake up laughing
into the cold so that the carriage shook
and never told why
it was always said that I was a happy child

the window over the street
the song of the trolley wires
from before

light singing along them
as I listened

it was the morning and it knew me
how did it find me

I was awake and watching and I remember

later when there were names it passed
all the way through them
coming going never turning
never in doubt though I grew older
and thought of differences
and moved away

and left the easel standing in the grass
at the top of the bank
facing the street
as though it were a mirror

the picture of bare day

the portrait of the light scarcely begun
as it would look when it found me

Earlier

Came from far up in the cool hour
from under the bridges the light
that was the river at that time
not a bird do I recall now
maybe never heard their voices
except the geese of the streetcars
stopping at the corner hissing
then the numb bell and the cello
rocking away into itself

one street east ran the avenue
on the cliffs facing the river
where I could see the light rising
from beyond the songs of the white tires
the teeth of roofs and the thin trees

and down there the harbor waited
in its tracks under messages
that shuffled across viaducts
between worlds never touched or smelled
their distant sounds motes in an eye

east of them flowed that hushed shining
recognizable yet unknown

Memorandum

Save these words for a while because
of something they remind you of
although you cannot remember
what that is a sense that is part
dust and part the light of morning

you were about to say a name
and it is not there I forget
them too I am learning to pray
to Perdita to whom I said
nothing at the time and now she
cannot hear me as far as I
know but the day goes on looking

the names often change more slowly
than the meanings whole families
grow up in them and then are gone
into the anonymous sky
oh Perdita does the hope go on
after the names are forgotten

and is the pain of the past done
when the calling has stopped and those
betrayals so long repeated
that they are taken for granted
as the shepherd does with the sheep

To *Echo*

What could they know of you
to be so sure of
that it frightened them
into passing judgment upon you
later from a distance

elusive wanderer *speaking*
when sound carries
over a river

or across a lake
recognized without being seen

beauty too far
beyond the human

then where did you go
do you go
to answer

often with voices
that once spoke for
the listeners

though only the last things

they called
ends of names greetings
the question Who

The Wild

First sight of water through trees
glimpsed as a child
and the smell of the lake then
on the mountain
how long it has lasted
whole and unmoved and without words
the sound native to a great bell
never leaving it

paw in the air
guide
ancient curlew not recorded
flying at night into
the age of night
sail sailing in the dark

so the tone of it
still crosses the years
through death after death
and the burnings the departures
the absences
carrying its own
song inside it

of bright water

Transit

Wyatt was on the way home
on a mission
trusted again more or less
but in a strange bed he died
Dante had gone the same way
never getting home with his breath

and with faces not known
clouding over them
what are you doing here
at the end of the world
words far from the tree
and the green season
of hearing

and not dying this time
or not planning to
but staying on with things to do

and eyes that can do nothing for you
by the tuned shore of dust
all of it lit from behind after singing

so soon

Usage

Do the words get old too
like all the things they are used for
which they follow trying
to keep in step with
to be the names of
to say what they are

shadows of wheat
in the waving wheat
a note waiting to be played
the small figure
appearing at last in the eyes
of statues
light moving over one face
words grow old without
speaking of such things
as long as they are there

only later
when the words are older
they start after
in another time

and what can they tell of age
itself
they that grow older
they that were always
older beyond knowing
when they say youth
youth
where is it every time

Home Tundra

It may be that the hour is snow
seeming never to settle not
even to be cold now slipping
away from underneath into
the past from which no sounds follow
what I hear is the dogs breathing
ahead of me in the shadow

two of them have already gone
far on into the dark of closed
pages out of sight and hearing
two of them are old already
one cannot hear one cannot see

even in sleep they are running
drawing me with them on their way
wrapped in a day I found today
we know where we are because we
are together here together
leaving no footprints in the hour

whatever the diaries say
nobody ever found the pole

Monologue

Heart
as we say
meaning it literally
and you do

hear it when
we speak
for the voice addressing you
is your own

though we know now
that the you
we are speaking to
is not the person
we imagine
yet we go on telling you

day after day of the person
we imagine
ourselves to be

forgetting as we tell you
learning even from joy
but forgetting
and you hear

who is speaking
you hear it all
though you do not listen

The Name of the Air

It could be like that then the beloved
old dog finding it harder and harder
to breathe and understanding but coming
to ask whether there is something that can
be done about it coming again to
ask and then standing there without asking

To Maoli as the Year Ends

Now that I think you no longer hear me
you go on listening to me
as you used to listen to music
old friend what are you hearing
that I do not hear though I listen
through the light of thirty thousand days
you still hear something that escapes me

The Flight of Language

Some of the leaves stay on all winter
and spring comes without knowing
whether there is suffering in them
or ever was
and what it is in the tongue they speak
that cannot be remembered by listening
for the whole time that they are on the tree
and then as they fly off with the air
that always through their lives was there

Heights

The dark morning says See how you forget

mountains camped by a stream
the chipped lake
gold strokes on the high
clawed hollows
where you never set foot

what would you see from there

not the past
which is fiction
nor the present which is the past

you would stand there shaken
in the presence of vertigo the god
clutching the air

hearing that one
note

you keep forgetting

This January

So after weeks of rain
at night the winter stars
that much farther in heaven
without our having seen them
in far light are still forming
the heavy elements
that when the stars are gone
fly up as dust finer
by many times than a hair
and recognize each other
in the dark traveling
at great speed and becoming
our bodies in our time
looking up after rain
in the cold night together

A Note About the Author

W. S. Merwin was born in New York City in 1927 and grew up in Union City, New Jersey, and Scranton, Pennsylvania. From 1949 to 1951 he worked as a tutor in France, Portugal, and Majorca. He has since lived in many parts of the world, most recently on Maui in the Hawaiian Islands, where he cultivates rare and endangered palm trees. His many works of poetry, prose, and translation are listed at the beginning of this volume. He has been awarded a fellowship of the Academy of American Poets (of which he is a former chancellor), the Pulitzer Prize, and the Bollingen Prize. Most recently, he has received the Governor's Award for Literature of the state of Hawaii, the Tanning Prize for mastery in the art of poetry, a Lila Wallace–Reader's Digest Writers' Award, and the Ruth Lilly Poetry Prize.

A Note on the Type

The text of this book was set in a typeface named Perpetua, designed by the British artist Eric Gill (1882–1940) and cut by the Monotype Corporation of London in 1928–30. Perpetua is a contemporary letter of original design, without any direct historical antecedents. The shapes of the roman letters basically derive from stonecutting, a form of lettering in which Gill was eminent. The italic is essentially an inclined roman. The general effect of the typeface in reading sizes is one of lightness and grace. The larger display sizes of the type are extremely elegant and form what is probably the most distinguished series of inscriptional letters cut in the present century.

Composed by Creative Graphics, Inc., Allentown, Pennsylvania

Printed and bound by United Book Press, Baltimore, Maryland

Designed by Iris Weinstein